Tacos Tempura and Teem Gok

A CHILD'S AMERICAN HERITAGE COOKBOOK
FEATURING SINGLE SERVING RECIPES

By

Nancy Lee

&

Linda Oldham

Cover Design Terry Smith   **Illustrations** Carol Angelo

We dedicate this book to our children: Lara, Karin, Chris, Sean, and Kirk. Together we have all learned to enjoy cooking as an avenue to understand and learn about others.

PRINTED IN THE UNITED STATES OF AMERICA

©1979 by Nancy Lee & Linda Oldham
ISBN # 0-931178-02-9
Library of Congress #-78-75120
Typeset by Century Composing
Printed by Delta Lithograph

CONTENTS

NEW IDEAS FROM HANDS ON PUBLICATIONS

NOTES TO YOUNG COOKS

This cookbook is a collection of recipes from seven cultures. You can make and taste dishes that are eaten by children like you from other parts of the world.

Some of the recipes are very easy, while others require more skill. If you are not an experienced cook, discuss the recipes with your mother before you begin to cook.

Always read the entire recipe before you begin and follow the rules of your kitchen.

1. Wash your hands.
2. Make sure that pot holders are ready for the handling of hot items.
3. Get all the ingredients and equipment out and ready before you begin to cook.
4. Be sure that an adult is nearby when you are near a heat source or using an electrical appliance.
5. When you finish cooking be sure that everything is turned off, cleaned, and put away.

THE COOKING OF CHINA

Modern Chinese cooking has evolved out of what were distinctly regional cooking styles. Due to the vastness of China and the great range of its climates, these styles were each unique. The five early styles were Peking, Honan, Szechwan, Canton and Fukien. Today four more general schools of cooking are referred to: northern (Peking, Shantung and Honan); coastal (Fukien and Shanghai); inland (Szechwan and Yunnan); and southern (the area around Canton).

Since China's history includes so much hunger and hardship, it is particularly admirable that the culture has developed its fine art of cooking. When a Chinese dish is prepared, more than just the sense of taste is considered. The colors must be pleasing to the eye, the ingredients must be of uniform size, and the food should have a pleasant aroma.

When a person is planning a meal, the dishes are chosen for contrasts in colors, textures, and tastes. A proper dinner includes one fowl, one fish, one meat dish and the appropriate vegetables. Desserts are practically unknown in China. In Chinese-American restaurants, however, this is not the case. Often a fortune cookie is served at the end of the meal.

ALMOND COOKIES - HSING-JEN-PING

Almond cookies are the traditional sweet offered in Chinese-American restaurants. The Chinese eat very few desserts immediately following a meal. Most of their sweets are served at tea time. In Northern Chinese cooking, pine nuts are frequently used. Substituting these for blanched almonds would also be good.

½ C.	(120ml.)	Flour
1/8 tsp.	(.6ml.)	Baking soda
3 Tbs.	(45ml.)	Sugar
¼ C.	(60ml.)	Shortening (lard is best)
1 Tbs.	(15ml.)	Beaten egg
¼ tsp.	(1.2ml.)	Almond extract

1 drop yellow food coloring
2 blanched almonds (cut in half lengthwise)

1. Sift flour and baking soda together.
2. Cream shortening and sugar.
3. Add the beaten egg and almond extract.
4. Mix thoroughly.
5. Gradually add the flour and soda mixture and mix well.
6. Roll a teaspoon of dough into a ball.
7. Press flat on ungreased cookie sheet.
8. Brush each cookie with beaten egg and press almond half into the center of each cookie.
9. Bake at 350°F, 176°C for 15-18 minutes.

6

FRIED WON TON

Fried Won Ton is an example of "deem sum". Deem sum means "touch the heart" or "dot heart" and implies a snack or appetizer.

2 Tbs.	(30ml.)	Chopped shrimp
¼ tsp.	(1.2ml.)	Minced parsley
¼ tsp.	(1.2ml.)	Chopped green onion
¼ tsp.	(1.2ml.)	Chopped water chestnuts
4 drops of pressed ginger or 1/8 tsp. (.6ml.) dried ginger		
½ tsp.	(2.4ml.)	Soy sauce
2 Won Ton skins		

1. Mix carefully the first 6 ingredients.
2. Place the shrimp mixture on the won ton skin.
3. Moisten 2 edges of the skin with water.
4. Fold skin in half to form a triangle.
5. Press edges to seal.
6. Deep fat fry 1 to 2 minutes at 370°F, 190°C.
7. Drain.

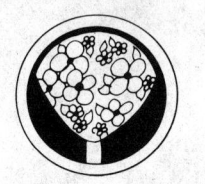

HOT CHILI BEEF FILLING FOR MANDARIN PANCAKES

BACKGROUND: Mandarin pancakes are usually filled with duck. Another variation is a chili filling, similar to the Mexican burrito. The proper way to fill and eat a Mandarin pancake is to spread the pancake on a plate. Then you put two to three Tbs. (30-45ml.) filling or Peking duck in the center. You roll the pancake up. You place the roll in your left hand if you are right-handed. This frees your right hand for the use of chopsticks on other dishes. Support the end of the pancake from underneath with your thumb and small finger.

1 lb.	(454gms.)	Boneless beef sirloin (cut in paper-thin strips)
3 Tbs.	(45ml.)	Soy sauce
1 Tbs.	(15ml.)	Sherry
2 tsp.	(10ml.)	Cornstarch
½ to 1 tsp.	(2.5 to 5ml.)	Liquid hot-pepper seasoning (optional)

1. Combine the soy sauce, sherry, cornstarch and hot pepper.
2. Add the meat and stir for a few minutes.
3. Heat 3 Tbs. (45ml.) oil over highest heat in fry pan.
4. Add meat mixture. (Be careful — this may splatter.)
5. Cook, stirring constantly, until meat looses pink color.
6. Place a little filling on Mandarin pancake, roll it up and fold one end up to hold in the pieces.

MANDARIN PANCAKES

The Mandarin Pancake is another example of the many kinds of flat bread found in cultures throughout the world. It has been called a Chinese tortilla.

¼ C.	(60ml.)	All-purpose flour
3 Tbs.	(45ml.)	Boiling water
Sesame oil or salad oil		

1. Put flour in margarine tub.
2. Add water and mix with chopsticks or a fork.
3. Work dough until it sticks together and then knead it on a lightly floured board or wax paper for 10 minutes until very smooth.
4. Cover and let stand for 30 minutes.
5. Cut the dough in half.
6. Shape each section into a ball and flatten slightly.
7. Roll each ball to 3" diameter on a lightly floured board.
8. Brush the top of one pancake with sesame oil and cover with the other pancake.
9. Press the two rounds lightly but firmly together to align them.
10. Roll the double pancake to 7" - 8" diameter on a lightly floured board.
11. Fry on a medium-high, ungreased frying pan turning every 15 seconds until pancake is blistered by air pockets, is slightly translucent, parchment colored and feels dry. Pancake should not brown; if overcooked, it becomes brittle.
12. Remove from pan and gently pull the two halves apart.

PAPER CHICKEN

This recipe represents the Chinese method of cooking in cellophane paper. This method is utilized to keep all the moisture in the meat and to keep out all the oil.

1" pieces of boned and skinned chicken (one chicken breast should be enough for twelve children)

2 tsp.	(10ml.)	Soy sauce
2 tsp.	(10ml.)	Sherry or chicken broth
2 tsp.	(10ml.)	Salad oil or sesame oil

Slivers of ginger root (optional)

¼ tsp.	(1.2ml.)	Grated fresh ginger

Cooking oil

6" squares of foil or parchment paper

1. Bone and skin chicken and cut into 1 x 1 x ½ inch slices.
2. Marinate pieces in soy sauce, broth, oil and ginger for 10 minutes.
3. Place one drained piece of chicken in the center of the foil.
4. Fold the foil over the chicken to form a triangle.
5. Very carefully seal the foil so that no oil can seep into the chicken.
6. Fry the packages for 2 minutes in deep oil at 350°F, 176°C.

RED BEAN POPSICLES - HUNG DOW BING

This is a very nutritious snack, because the red beans are healthful. The red beans are available only in Asian markets. If you are lucky enough to have this resource, you will love this snack.

1 lb.	(.45kilo)	Smooth red beans (available in Asian markets)
Water to cover beans		
½ C.	(120ml.)	Brown sugar (more if you prefer a sweeter taste)
Popsicle sticks		

1. Wash and drain beans.
2. Put in a large pot and cover with water.
3. Bring to boil, then add the sugar.
4. Cover pot, turn heat to low and simmer 2½ to 3 hours.
5. Allow the beans to cool slightly, then pour the mixture through a fine sieve into a large bowl.
6. Transfer to an ice cube tray and place in freezer.
7. When the mixture starts to congeal, insert popsicle sticks.

SINGING RICE

This rice snaps, crackles and pops when hot food is poured over it. Legend says that a chef invented it from leftovers when he had to feed an emperor unexpectedly. The dish was such a success that the chef was hired to cook for the emperor's court.

1 C.	(240ml.)	Long grain rice
4 C.	(960ml.)	Water
2 tsp.	(10ml.)	Salt
Salad oil for deep frying		

1. A day in advance put rice, water and salt in a two-quart saucepan. Let stand one half hour.
2. Bring to boil, cover and simmer thirty minutes.
3. Drain.
4. Spread evenly on a heavily greased cookie sheet.
5. Bake at 250°F, 121°C for 8 hours, turn rice occasionally with spatula.
6. Deep fry at 425°F, 218°C for 4 minutes.
7. Drain.
8. Transfer to warm serving platter or soup bowl.
9. Pour hot soup or entree over rice at table. (Rice, food and containers must be hot for rice to sing.)

SPRING ROLLS (OR PANCAKE ROLLS)

Spring rolls are soft pancakes offered to the diner, who then chooses the filling from a variety of foods laid out in front of him. He fills his pancake with the ingredients of his choice and rolls it up (turning up and in on one end). The fillings are usually shredded cooked meats and quick-fried crunchy vegetables. The pancakes get their name because they are served most often in the spring when the vegetables are best.

Because preparing spring-roll wrappers from scratch is such a precise culinary operation, we suggest that you use the ready-made variety. These are available at a Chinese market.

1 Tbs.	(15ml.)	Lard or shortening
¼ lb.	(.11kilo)	Shredded pork
¼ lb.	(.11kilo)	Bean sprouts
2 Spring onions (cut in 1" segments)		
1 Tbs.	(15ml.)	Soy sauce
1 tsp.	(5ml.)	Sugar
6 Spring-roll wrappers		

1. Heat shortening in frying pan.
2. Add the pork and stir-fry for 2 minutes.
3. Add all other ingredients except wrappers and stir-fry for 2 minutes.
4. Place an equal portion on each of the wrappers.
5. Roll from the bottom two thirds of the way, then roll the rest of way.
6. Moisten edge with beaten egg and press down.
7. Deep fry the rolls in hot oil for about three minutes.
8. Drain.

13

TEEM GOK

Teem Gok is an example of "deem sum". Deem sum means "touch the heart", or "dot heart", and implies a snack or appetizer.

INGREDIENTS:

¼ tsp.	(1.2ml.)	Brown sugar
¼ tsp.	(1.2ml.)	White sugar
¼ tsp.	(1.2ml.)	Coconut meal
2 peanuts, chopped		
Won ton skins		
Oil		

1. Mix the first four ingredients.
2. Place mixture in center of won ton skin.
3. Moisten two adjacent edges with water.
4. Fold skin into triangle.
5. Seal the moistened edges.
6. Fry in hot oil for one minute at 375°F, 190°C.
7. Drain.

INTRODUCING THE COOKING OF GREECE

Ancient Greeks are thought to have begun the art of cooking nearly 3,000 years ago. A Greek, Archestratus, wrote the first cook book more than 2,000 years ago and Greek cooking has influenced many different cuisines. Today, Greek, Turkish, and Armenian dishes are often similar and it is difficult to determine the origin of these recipes because the borders of these countries have changed many times.

There are many olive and lemon trees in Greece, therefore olives and lemons are used extensively in Greek cooking. Every-day meals are generally simple. Often a complete meal will be fresh vegetables quickly cooked, sprinkled with olive oil and lemon juice. Delicious feasts presented elegantly are also a part of the Greek cooking heritage.

Kali Orexi means Good appetite!

BAKLAVA

Greeks rarely eat dessert after dinner. They prefer their sweets, pastries and rich desserts during the early evening (about 5:00 P.M.). Many Greek desserts are soaked overnight in syrup or honey. Baklava is the best-known example of this type of Greek dessert. It is made from filo which is a paper-thin pastry dough made with salt, flour, water and skill. Filo is available in Greek markets.

9"x9" square of filo		
1 tsp.	(5ml.)	Crushed nuts
		Melted margarine

Syrup:

2½ C.	(600ml.)	Sugar
2 C.	(480ml.)	Water
		Juice of 1 lemon

1. The syrup must be cold when it is poured on the hot baklava, so it should be made first and refrigerated.
2. Combine the sugar, water and lemon, bring to a boil and simmer for 10 minutes. Refrigerate.
3. Fold filo in thirds to form strip.
4. Brush filo with melted margarine.
5. Place one heaping teaspoon of crushed walnuts at one end of filo strip.
6. Fold nuts into filo. Use a triangle fold. Keep nuts inside.
7. Place triangle on baking pan and brush top with melted margarine.
8. Bake at 375°F, 190°C for 15 minutes.
9. Soak hot Baklava in approximately 2 Tbs. (30ml.) cold syrup for 5 minutes, turning frequently.

DRACHMA FRIED POTATOES

Most meals ordered in Greece come with these potatoes, cut into round shapes like the Greek silver coin, the drachma.

¼ to ½		Potato
2 C.	(480ml.)	Oil for frying
		Salt

1. Peel the potatoes and slice into ½ inch rounds.
2. Dry with towel.
3. Heat oil in a large frying pan until hot.
4. Gently place potatoes in oil and fry 10 minutes or until ready. For very crisp potatoes, fry only 5 minutes. Remove from oil and place in refrigerator to chill. Reheat oil until hot again and place chilled, partially cooked potatoes in oil to finish frying for 5 minutes more.
5. Use slotted spoon to turn potatoes over and remove from oil.
6. Drain on paper towels.
7. Sprinkle with salt while hot.

EGG AND LEMON SAUCE (SALTSA AVGOLEMONO)

BACKGROUND: The Greeks use a lot of lemon and olive oil in their cooking. Often a complete meal will be fresh vegetables, quickly cooked and served with a lemon sauce. A typical sauce used to enhance vegetables is made from the water the vegetables were cooking in, enriched with olive oil, thickened with egg yolks and spiced with lemon. The following recipe is an easy-to-make version of this white sauce that could be used for the children to dip vegetables.

INGREDIENTS:

4 egg yolks		
3 to 4 Tbs.	(45-60ml.)	Lemon juice
3 to 4 Tbs.	(45-60ml.)	Hot seasoned broth

PROCEDURE:

1. Beat egg yolks until thick.
2. Slowly beat in lemon juice, then the hot broth.
3. Cook over very low heat, stirring constantly, until thickened and smooth.
4. Turn off heat, cover pan, let stand 5 minutes.
5. If a thinner sauce is desired, add more broth. Makes ½ cup (120ml.)

GREEK SALAD

Greek meals usually include large salads which are frequently prepared at table. Often the greens are omitted from the salad.

¼ C.	(60ml.)	Chicory
¼ C.	(60ml.)	Romaine
1 Tbs.	(15ml.)	Cucumber, peeled and diced
1 Tbs.	(15ml.)	Tomatoes, diced
1 sliced radish (optional)		
1 Greek olive		
1 tsp.	(5ml.)	Green onion, chopped
1 Tbs.	(15ml.)	Olive oil
1½ tsp.	(7.5ml.)	Red wine vinegar or lemon
Pinch of salt and pepper mixture		
Pinch of oregano		
1 Anchovy fillet		
½ oz.	(15 gms.)	Feta cheese, crumbled

1. Chop all the vegetables.
2. Combine the vegetables in a margarine tub.
3. Combine the olive oil, red wine vinegar or lemon, salt, pepper and oregano. Shake or stir this dressing.
4. The anchovy fillet can be ground and included in dressing, chopped and put in salad or omitted.
5. Crumble the feta cheese on top of the salad.
6. Toss and enjoy.

HALVAH

It is often difficult to determine if a particular dish (recipe) is of Greek, Turkish, or Armenian origin because the borders of these countries have changed many times and the dishes are very similar. The Turks are thought to have brought Halvah to Greece in the 1300's. Halvah is used extensively in Jewish households in the United States.

1/3 C.	(80ml.)	Olive oil
1 C.	(240ml.)	Semolina or white cornmeal
2/3 C.	(160ml.)	Sugar
1 C.	(240ml.)	Milk
1/3 C.	(80ml.)	Water

1. In a heavy saucepan, heat the oil over moderate heat until a light haze forms above it.
2. Slowly pour in the semolina a thin stream, stirring constantly.
3. Reduce the heat to low and simmer for 20 minutes, or until all the oil has been absorbed and the meal turns a light golden color, stirring occasionally.
4. Add the sugar, stirring constantly
5. Gradually stir in the milk and water mixture.
6. Continue cooking about 10 minutes longer, stirring constantly until the mixture is thick enough to hold its shape almost solidly in the spoon.
7. Pour the halvah into a small (3"x 5") ungreased baking dish, spread it and smooth the top with the back of a spoon.
8. Cool until firm and then cut into 1" squares.

KOULOURAKIA

Koulourakia is a Greek Easter sweet that is a shortbread cookie decorated with sesame seeds. It may be coiled or shaped like a pretzel.

1 Tbs.	(15ml.)	Butter
1 Tbs plus 1 tsp.	(20ml.)	Sugar
1½ tsp.	(7.5ml.)	Beaten egg yolks
1 tsp.	(5ml.)	Light cream
1/8 tsp.	(.6ml.)	Vanilla
¼ C.	(60ml.)	Unsifted all-purpose flour
1/8 tsp.	(.6ml.)	Baking powder
Pinch of nutmeg or cinnamon		

1. Cream together the butter and sugar.
2. Add the beaten egg yolks, cream and vanilla.
3. Combine the flour, baking powder and nutmeg or cinnamon and add to the mixture.
4. Mix well, cover and chill until the dough is easy to work with (approximately 15 minutes).
5. Roll the dough into a coil and shape.
6. Brush top with beaten egg white and sprinkle with sesame seeds.
7. Bake at 350°F, 176°C, 8 - 10 minutes.

LAMB IN A BAG

Ancient Greek sheepherders wrapped their meat in paper (klephtiko) to seal in the cooking odors so their enemies, the Turks, would not find them.

1" square piece of lamb
1 pinch mixture of salt, pepper, oregano, garlic powder and grated lemon peel
1" square piece zucchini cut lengthwise
1" square piece crookneck squash cut lengthwise
1 Mushroom

¼ tsp.	(1.2ml.)	Lemon juice
1 tsp.	(5ml.)	Melted butter

1 Small paper bag or 9" square piece of paper
Salad oil to coat outside of paper bag

1. Coat outside of bag or piece of paper with salad oil.
2. Season the lamb with the salt, pepper, and spice mixture and place in the bag or on paper.
3. Mix the lemon juice and melted butter.
4. Roll the vegetables in the lemon butter and place in bag or on piece of paper.
5. Fold down bag or fold paper and secure with paper clip.
6. Place bag or folded paper on baking pan and bake at 350°F, 176°C, 15 minutes.

SOUPA AVGOLEMONO (LEMON SOUP)

Greece produces large flavorful lemons and Greek cooks use them in a variety of ways. They generously season their vegetables and salads with them. In salads, the lemon is used in place of salad dressing vinegar. The following recipe is for a lemon-flavored chicken soup called soupa avgolemono — this is the national soup of Greece.

4 cans or 48 oz.	(1440ml. or 1.5 liters)	Chicken broth
3 Tbs.	(45ml.)	Uncooked rice
3		Eggs, beaten
3 Tbs.	(45ml.)	Lemon juice

1. Cook broth and rice until the rice is tender, about twenty minutes.
2. Beat eggs until they are light and gradually add lemon juice, beating until blended.
3. Pour part of the hot soup slowly into the egg mixture.
4. Return this mixture to the remainder of the soup.

This recipe serves six.

LENTIL SOUP AND FASSOULADA SOUP

Due to the abundant supplies of olive trees, olives are a large part of the Greek diet and olive oil is used extensively in their cooking. The two following soup recipes are common dishes that utilize olive oil.

LENTIL SOUP (FAHKEE)

3/4 C.	(180ml.)	Lentils
3½ C.	(840ml.)	Water
½ C.	(120ml.)	Tomato sauce
½ tsp.	(2.5ml.)	Salt
2½ Tbs.	(37.5ml.)	Olive oil
2 cloves		Garlic, unpeeled

1. Empty the lentils into a dish. Look them over and remove any gravel.
2. Put the lentils into a saucepan, rinse with cold running water and drain.
3. Add the 3½ cups water and the garlic.
4. Bring to a boil. Turn to low heat, stir in the tomato sauce, salt, and olive oil.
5. Simmer gently for 50 minutes. Add water if the soup becomes too thick.
Serves three.

FASSOULADA SOUP (NATIONAL BEAN SOUP)

1 lb.	(454 grams)	Dried navy beans
2		Large onions, sliced or chopped
2		Garlic cloves, crushed
½ C.	(120ml.)	Olive oil
¼ tsp.	(1.2ml.)	Thyme
1 Tbs.	(15ml.)	Tomato paste
2 tsp.	(10ml.)	Salt
		Freshly ground black pepper
4 Qts.	(4.5 liters)	Boiling water (to cover)
		Juice of half a lemon
2 Tbs.	(30ml.)	Minced parsley

1. Soak the beans overnight; drain.
2. Cook the onions and crushed garlic in olive oil until they are transparent, add thyme and tomato paste.
3. Add the drained beans, salt, pepper, and enough water to stand at least two inches above the top of the beans.
4. Cook slowly, covered, 2 to 3 hours, until beans are very soft.
5. Shortly before serving, add lemon juice and parsley.

Serves eight people.

NEW YEAR'S BREAD (VASILOPETA)

This Greek New Year's bread is a large loaf of sweet bread formed from several little balls. Blanched almonds are poked into the dough to form the numeral of the new year. It is customary to bake a coin in each loaf and slice the bread at midnight. Whoever gets the coin is blessed with good fortune in the new year.

¾ tsp.	(3.7ml.)	Active dry yeast
1 Tbs.	(15ml.)	Warm water
1 Tbs.	(15ml.)	Milk
1 Tbs.	(15ml.)	Butter
3 Tbs.	(45ml.)	Beaten egg
1 1/3 Tbs.	(20ml.)	Sugar
½ tsp.	(2.5ml.)	Grated orange peel
1 pinch		Nutmeg
1 pinch		Salt
¾ C.	(180ml.)	Unsifted all-purpose flour

1. Combine the yeast with the warm water and stir to dissolve.
2. Add the next seven ingredients and stir well.
3. Add the flour slowly to the liquid, use a little less or a little more than ¾ cup flour to make the dough a workable consistency.
4. Knead the dough on a floured board for five minutes, cover and let rise for one hour in a warm place.
5. Punch down and knead again.
6. Make ½" balls and form a loaf.
7. Cover and let rise for twenty minutes in a warm place.
8. Brush top with egg yolk mixed with 1 Tbs. (15ml.) water.
9. Decorate with sesame seeds and blanched almonds.
10. Bake at 350°F, 176°C for 15 minutes.

PATATOKEFTEHES (POTATO PANCAKES)

Many different cultures make potato pancakes with a few variations. In Israel, potato pancakes are called Latkes.

½ C.	(120ml.)	Cold mashed potatoes
2 Tbs.	(30ml.)	Beaten egg
1 tsp.	(5ml.)	Chopped onion or scallion
2¼ tsp.	(11.2ml.)	Flour
¼ tsp.	(1.2ml.)	Parsley
1 pinch		Salt
¼ C.	(60ml.)	Grated cheese, Kefaloteri or Parmesan
½ C.	(120ml.)	Oil, for frying OR use 1 cube of melted butter, if broiling or baking.

1. Mix all ingredients in a margarine tub except fats and cheese.
2. Make patties.
3. Dip in grated cheese.
4. Fry in hot oil until brown on both sides, about 10 minutes.
5. Use a wide spatula to turn over.
6. If broiling or baking is preferred, lay patties in buttered pan, sprinkle with grated cheese and bake at 450°F, 232°C for 15 minutes, or broil until brown for approximately 10 minutes.
7. Serve plain, with yogurt or garlic sauce.

TIROPETES

Vasilopitta is a Greek holiday celebrated in January, that in English means St. Basil's pie. The holiday is observed in churches and among families, where special pies made from filo dough, eggs and cheese are served. Each pie contains a coin, and the person who finds it in his slice is thought to be lucky for the whole year.

9x9 inch square of filo (available in a Greek market)
Melted butter or margarine

1 Tbs.	(15ml.)	Feta cheese
1 Tbs.	(15ml.)	Small curd cottage cheese
1 Tbs.	(15ml.)	Cream cheese
1½ tsp.	(7.5ml.)	Beaten egg
¼ tsp.	(1.2ml.)	Chopped parsley
¼ tsp.	(1.2ml.)	Chopped chives

1. Cream together the feta, cottage cheese and cream cheese.
2. Add the beaten egg, parsley and chives and mix well.
3. Fold two pieces of filo in thirds to form strips.
4. Brush filo with melted margarine.
5. Place one heaping Tbs. (15ml.) cheese-egg mixture at one end of filo strip. (Add coin if desired.)
6. Fold the cheese mixture into filo. Use a triangle fold.
7. Place triangle on greased baking sheet and brush top with melted margarine.
8. Bake at 375°F, 190°C for 15 minutes.

THE COOKING OF ISRAEL

Tzenna (meaning austerity) is the word for food in Israel. Israeli cooking really had its origin in 1948 when Israel came into existence. People of at least eighty nationalities have come together to form the population of Israel, each bringing their recipes and traditions from the lands they left.

Israeli cooking is lumped into three categories: European, Oriental (which covers non-European dishes: Arabic, North African, Indian, and the Far East), and original dishes.

Israelis are developing original dishes, neither European nor Oriental, that utilize the plentiful products that are grown in their country. Due to modern farming techniques, Israeli farmers have increased production six-fold in the past two decades. Israel is the third largest exporter of avocados (after California and South Africa). They also raise guava, citrus fruits, mangos, vegetables, dates, rice and honey.

BAGEL COOKIES (KA'ACHEI SUMSUM)

BACKGROUND: Bagels are traditional food eaten by Jews throughout the world. These bagels are usually eaten for Sabbath breakfast, with coffee, by Syrian Jews in Israel.

1 tsp.	(5ml.)	Yeast
¼ tsp.	(1.2ml.)	Sugar
2 Tbs.	(30ml.)	Warm water
½ C.	(120ml.)	Flour
2 Tbs.	(30ml.)	Melted margarine
1/8 tsp.	(.6ml.)	Salt
		One beaten egg
3 oz.	(80ml.)	Sesame seeds

1. Place yeast and sugar in a bowl.
2. Pour over water and stir to dissolve. Place in a warm place for 10 minutes.
3. Mix flour, salt, margarine and yeast mixture to form a dough.
4. Cover dough with a towel. Put in a warm place for 2 hours.
5. After dough rises, take small ball and roll into strips 4 inches (10cm.) long.
6. Form into bagel or doughnut shape, moisten ends if needed to join ends.
7. Place on greased baking sheet.
8. Brush with beaten egg, sprinkle with sesame seeds.
9. Bake at 375°F, 190°C, for 20-30 minutes.

CHALLAH BREAD (BRAIDED BREAD)

Challah is the traditional twisted bread always served on the Sabbath. An old tradition that goes back to the time when loaves were carried as a tribute to the priests in the Temple in Jerusalem, is that the person baking the bread breaks off a bit of dough and throws it in the fire while saying a prayer for their home and for peace for the world.

1 tsp.	(5ml.)	Dry yeast
1 Tbs.	(15ml.)	Warm water
¼ C.	(60ml.)	Hot water
1 tsp.	(5ml.)	Vegetable oil
½ tsp.	(2.5ml.)	Salt
½ tsp.	(2.5ml.)	Sugar
1 Tbs.	(15ml.)	Beaten egg
1 C.	(240ml.)	Flour

1. Soften the yeast in the warm water.
2. To the boiling hot water, add the oil, salt and sugar. Stir until the sugar is dissolved.
3. Cool and when lukewarm, add the softened yeast.
4. Add the beaten egg to the liquid.
5. Add enough flour and stir and beat to make a smooth, thick batter.
6. Let sit for a few minutes (approximately 10) then add the rest of the flour to make a dough that can be handled.
7. Knead until smooth and elastic on wax paper.
8. Shape into a ball and grease the surface, place in a greased bowl and cover with a clean cloth.
9. Let rise in a warm place, until doubled in size.
10. Knead again until dough is fine-grained.
11. Divide dough into 3 portions.
12. Roll each into long strips and fasten ends together. Braid into a twisted loaf.
13. Place loaf on a greased baking sheet.
14. Cover and let rise until double in bulk again in a warm place.
15. Brush top with beaten egg with 1tsp. (5 ml.) cold water added and sprinkle with poppy seeds.
16. Bake in a hot oven at 375°F, 190°C for 10-12 minutes; then at 350°F, 176°C for 15 minutes.

FALAFEL

Falafel is as common in Israel as the hot dog is in the United States. It is sold on many street corners throughout the country. It consists of chick-pea balls served in Pita bread with lettuce, tomato, and a sauce.

3 Tbs.	(45ml.)	Chick-peas (soak 12-24 hours and drain, or washed and drained canned beans may be used)
1 inch	(2.5cm.)	Piece of green onion
½ tsp.	(2.5ml.)	Beaten egg
1/8 tsp.	(.6ml.)	Lemon juice
2 tsp.	(10ml.)	Cracked wheat soaked (soak bulgar wheat 12-24 hours, drain)
2 drops		Crushed garlic
Pinch		Salt
Pinch		Red pepper

1. Grind the chick-peas and green onion with a fine grinder.
2. Add the egg, lemon juice, cracked wheat, garlic, salt, pepper and mix well.
3. Form 3 balls, roll them in wheat flour.
4. Deep-fry at 375°F, 190°C for 1-2 minutes.
5. Drain.
6. Eat by themselves, or place in Pita bread with lettuce, tomatoes, and sauce.

FRUIT FRITTERS

There are many varieties of latkes made in different countries, also there are many varieties enjoyed during the Chanukah season. In addition to the cheese, potato, and just plain latkes, Israelis also make fruit fritters. The batter is especially delicate, similar to a Japanese tempura, and the fruit may be any kind that is in season.

INGREDIENTS:

¼ C.	(60ml.)	Flour
½ tsp.	(2.5ml.)	Baking powder
Pinch		Salt
1¼ tsp.	(6.2ml.)	Sugar
1 Tbs.	(15ml.)	Beaten egg
2 Tbs.	(30ml.)	Milk
1 tsp.	(5ml.)	Melted margarine
		Sliced bananas, apples or other fruit

PROCEDURE:
1. Sift together flour, baking powder, salt and sugar.
2. Mix the egg, milk and melted margarine.
3. Stir the liquid mixture into the dry ingredients.
4. Blend until smooth but do not overbeat.
5. Batter should be heavy enough to coat the fruit; adjust with more milk or flour, if necessary.
6. Dip fruit into batter and deep-fry in hot fat.
7. Drain on paper towels.
8. Usually are served with confectioners' sugar sprinkled on top.

HAMANTASCHEN

Hamantaschen are triangularly shaped, filled cookies that are traditionally served at the feast of Purim. Purim is a spring holiday celebrating the freeing of ancient Jews from the Persian prime minister Haman, who was going to have them killed. The Hamantaschen are shaped like a triangle because the wicked Haman wore a three-cornered hat.

Pastry:

2 Tbs.	(30ml.)	Beaten egg
2 Tbs.	(30ml.)	Sugar
2 Tbs.	(30ml.)	Melted butter
1½ tsp.	(7.5ml.)	Water
¼ tsp.	(1.2ml.)	Vanilla
1 Tbs.	(15ml.)	Lemon juice
1/8 tsp.	(.6ml.)	Baking soda
1/8 tsp.	(.6ml.)	Baking powder
Pinch		Salt
¾ C.	(180ml.)	Flour

Filling:

¼ C.	(60ml.)	Lekvar (Prune butter)
2 Tbs.	(30ml.)	Chopped nuts
½ tsp.	(2.5ml.)	Grated lemon rind

34

1. Preheat oven to 375°F, 190°C and grease cookie sheet.
2. Put beaten eggs in margarine tub then beat in sugar, butter, water, vanilla and lemon juice.
3. Sift flour with baking soda, baking powder and salt.
4. Slowly add the flour mixture to the liquid mixture. Mix together until the dough forms a ball and seems stiff enough to be rolled out. Wrap dough and cool while you make filling.
5. To make filling, combine the prune mixture, lemon and nuts and mix well.
6. Put dough on a lightly floured piece of wax paper, then roll out dough until quite thin.
7. Cut out circles of dough with a cutter or the edge of a glass.
8. Place rounded tsp. (5ml.) of filling in center of dough circle.
9. Loosen dough by slipping table knife under three sides, flip dough over filling forming a triangle.
10. Pinch all seams of dough, sealing filling inside.
11. Place Hamantaschen on greased cookie sheet. Drip ¼ to ½ tsp. (1.2-2.5ml.) honey over top of each.
12. Bake until golden, about 12 minutes at 375°F, 190°C.

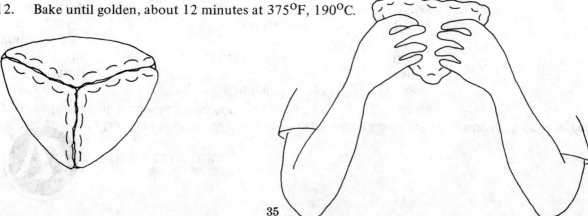

HONEY CLUSTERS

The people of Israel come from many other lands yet all celebrate their New Year by eating foods that are cooked with honey.

¼ C.	(60ml.)	Flour
Pinch		Salt
1 Tbs.	(15ml.)	Beaten egg

Syrup:

½ C.	(120ml.)	Honey
¼ tsp.	(1.2ml.)	Ginger

1. Sift the flour.
2. Mix the flour, egg and salt.
3. Knead the dough, adding more flour if it is too sticky.
4. Roll the dough into a rope 1/3" thick.
5. Cut into ½" pieces and place them on a well greased cookie sheet.
6. Bake at 375°F, 190°C for 15 minutes or until golden brown, turn the pieces with a spatula to brown both sides evenly.
7. Bring the honey and ginger to a boil in a saucepan.
8. Add the baked pieces and boil gently for 20 minutes, stirring with a wooden spoon.
9. Remove from syrup and place on a slightly greased plate.
10. Allow to cool before eating.

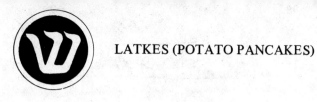

LATKES (POTATO PANCAKES)

Potato pancakes are made in a variety of ways in several cultures. A recipe for Greek potato pancakes (patatokeftehes) can be found on page 27. Applesauce is usually served with Latkes.

½ C.	(120ml.)	Grated potato
1 Tbs.	(15ml.)	Grated onion
Pinch		Salt and pepper
1 tsp.	(5ml.)	Matzo meal
1 Tbs.	(15ml.)	Beaten egg
		Vegetable oil for cooking

PROCEDURE:
1. Peel and grate the potatoes and onion.
2. Drain the mixture by placing it in a towel and pressing the liquid out.
3. Place the potato-onion mixture in a margarine tub.
4. Add the salt, pepper, matzo meal and egg.
5. Mix vigorously until the ingredients are well combined.
6. Heat cooking oil in a heavy skillet until a drop of water sputters and evaporates instantly.
7. Drop 1-2 Tbs. (15-30ml.) batter into skillet and flatten it into a 2-2½" cake.
8. Fry about 2 minutes on each side, or until they are golden brown.

PITA BREAD

Pita bread is a flat bread used extensively in Middle Eastern cooking. It is frequently filled with various stuffings and eaten like a sandwich.

1 scant tsp.	(4ml.)	Dry yeast
¼ C.	(60ml.)	Warm water
1/8 tsp.	(.6ml.)	Salt
½ C.	(120ml.)	Flour

1. Sprinkle the yeast on the warm water and stir to dissolve.
2. Add salt.
3. Add the flour slowly, beating vigorously.
4. Knead the dough on a well-floured board for four minutes with greased hands.
5. Flatten dough into two 4" circles on a greased cookie sheet.
6. Cover with towel and let rise 25 minutes.
7. Bake at 475°F, 246°C 12-15 minutes.

POPPYSEED CANDY

Poppyseeds are used frequently in Israeli candies and cookies.

¼ C.	(60ml.)	Poppy seed
½ C.	(120ml.)	Honey
2 Tbs.	(30ml.)	Nuts

1. Rinse the poppy seeds in a fine strainer. Drain well.
2. Chop the nuts.
3. Place the seeds, honey and nuts in a small saucepan and bring to a boil over medium heat.
4. Boil steadily for 8 minutes; if mixture browns sooner, remove from heat.
5. Spread mixture on a greased plate.
6. Cut into squares while still hot.
7. It will be chewy when cool.

INTRODUCING THE COOKING OF JAPAN

To the Japanese, food is seen as an esthetic experience. One of the most important aspects of Japanese cooking is the manner in which the food is served. Great emphasis is placed on the table decor, arrangements and appearance of the food. For generations it has been the informal custom to eat and serve their food in a particular order: mountain products first, then sea products, next field products, and finally products of the towns. Busy people of the twentieth century have changed this practice but try to keep the spirit of it. For example, in sashimi, the ingredients are arranged in a design representing the landscape of a hill, field and water. Meals are also planned according to the season. For example, hot meals, particularly nabemono(s) (one-pot cooking) are served during winter; cold or room temperature meals such as sashimi, sushi or chilled sunomono are served during hot weather.

Limited access to foods, especially meat, has caused the Japanese cooks to develop many varied ways to prepare the same foods (pickling, steaming, deep frying, pan frying, etc.). Menus offer many variations according to the limitations of the geography or agricultural offerings; however, there are certain items that are served at almost every meal. There is nearly always at least one soup with each meal. Hot, plain, boiled rice is served at every meal, except when noodles or another rice dish is the main course. Tsukemono, or pickles, are served at most meals. The Japanese enjoy pickles so much that it is a typical dessert and it is often served at breakfast with hot rice.

The Japanese feel that the touch of a metal utensil to the mouth is unpleasant and therefore use chopsticks. Today in Japan, both Eastern and Western foods are enjoyed. When spaghetti, hamburgers, eggs and salads are eaten, they use knives and forks instead of chopsticks.

CHICKEN BAKED IN SILVER FOIL (TORI NO GIN-GAMI YAKI)

In Japan today classic Nipponese cooking has blended with the styles of China, Europe and America, and a unique and varied style of cooking has developed. This recipe of chicken baked in foil is an adaptation of the Chinese paper chicken.

1" Piece of boned, skinned chicken
1 Fresh mushroom, sliced
1" Piece of sweet potato, cut into thickness of a pencil
1 tsp.   (5ml.)   Grated cheese
Butter
Cellophane or wax paper — 6" square
Aluminum foil — 6" square

1. Prepare the chicken, vegetables and cheese.
2. Lay out the sheet of aluminum foil; over this lay the sheet of cellophane (wax paper).
3. Lightly butter the surface of the cellophane (wax paper).
4. Arrange the chicken, mushroom, and sweet potato on the buttered cellophane (wax paper).
5. Sprinkle with the grated cheese.
6. Fold over the cellophane (wax paper) then fold up the aluminum foil, encasing the cellophane tightly.
7. Bake at 375°F, 190°C for fifteen minutes.

 EGG ROLL

These Japanese egg rolls are not at all like Chinese egg rolls. They are not covered with pancake-like skins, instead they are more like a pancake that is rolled. These could be compared to the latkes or patatokeftehes.

1 oz.	(30gms.)	Halibut or Sole (Precooked)
1½ tsp.	(7.5ml.)	Sugar
1		Egg
2 tsp.	(10ml.)	Clam juice
1 tsp.	(5ml.)	Soy sauce
1 tsp.	(5ml.)	Sherry
2 Tbs.	(30ml.)	Oil
Pinch		Salt

1. Heat the oil in the skillet to 350°F, 176°C.
2. Flake the fish with a fork.
3. Beat the egg in a margarine tub and combine with the fish.
4. Add the sugar, clam juice, soy sauce, sherry and salt.
5. Pour the mixture into the pan and fry until lightly browned on both sides.
6. Remove from pan and roll like a jelly roll.
7. Let cool five minutes, then slice in one inch pieces.

EGG SOUP

Soup is a part of almost every Japanese meal. There are two basic types, suimono (clear soup) and miso-shiru (soy bean paste soup).

1 Tbs.	(15ml.)	Cornstarch
1 C.	(240ml.)	Beef broth
1 C.	(240ml.)	Clam juice
1 tsp.	(5ml.)	Soy sauce
1		Egg
1 Tbs.	(15ml.)	Chopped scallions

1. Mix the cornstarch with a small amount of the broth.
2. Add soy sauce and the rest of the broth and clam juice.
3. Boil gently.
4. Beat the egg and slowly pour it onto the surface of the boiling broth.
5. Cook until the eggs are set.
6. Sprinkle on the scallions when serving.

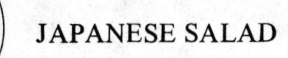

JAPANESE SALAD

Most Japanese salads include as main ingredients cucumbers and seafood, because both items are abundant.

1¼ tsp.	(6.2ml.)	Vinegar
1/3 C.	(80ml.)	Soy sauce
¼ tsp.	(1.2ml.)	Grated fresh ginger or ½ tsp. (2.5ml.) cut up crystallized ginger.
1		Large cucumber, sliced
½ C.	(120ml.)	Cooked shrimp

1. If you use crystallized ginger, wash the sugar off the slices, dry them, and cut them into small pieces.
2. In a cup, mix the vinegar, soy sauce and ginger.
3. In a cereal bowl, mix the cucumbers and shrimp.
4. Cover shrimp and cucumbers with soy sauce dressing.

SUKIYAKI

In Japan sukiyaki is known as the "friendship dish". The ingredients are sliced uniformly and arranged beautifully on a platter. The cooking is done in an orderly ritualistic manner.

1 lb.	(.45kilo.)	Thinly sliced sirloin tip
1		Onion
1 Bunch		Green onions
6		Large fresh mushrooms
1 Can		Bamboo shoots (drained)
½ lb.	(.23kilo.)	Fresh spinach
6 ribs		Celery or Chinese cabbage
1 can		Shirataki (spaghetti-shaped yam shreds, drained) or 2 C. (480ml.) bean sprouts
½ C.	(120ml.)	Soy sauce
½ C.	(120ml.)	Stock
1 tsp.	(5ml.)	Sugar
½ tsp.	(2.5ml.)	MSG
3 Tbs.	(45ml.)	Cooking oil

1. Put the suet or cooking oil in a skillet over medium heat.
2. Saute the beef slices in the oil, turn frequently and do not allow the meat to brown, approximately three minutes.
3. Push the meat to one side and saute the vegetables. Add them in sequence beginning with the vegetables that require longer cooking.
4. First saute the onions until they are golden.
5. As you add the green onions, mushrooms, bamboo shoots, spinach and celery pour in the soy sauce and stock mixture a little at a time.
6. Sprinkle the sugar and MSG over the vegetables while you are stir-frying them.
7. The sauteing of vegetables from onions through celery should take about seven minutes.
8. Push the meat into the center of the skillet, add the shiritaki or sprouts, and heat and stir for about four more minutes.
9. You may serve this mixture in a well-beaten raw egg. Boiled rice is often served to compliment this dish.

SUSHI

Sushi is centuries old and one of the most authentic Japanese dishes you can experience. Of the Japanese culinary arts, sushi is probably the most refined in visual artistry and taste. There are several varieties of sushi. Nigiri is a small mound of rice flavored with vinegar and sugar. It may be topped with raw fish. Maki-zushi is made by wrapping the flavored rice with seaweed. Inari-zushi is the same type of rice wrapped in a deep-fried bean cake.

3 or 4 C.	(720ml. or 960ml.)	Cooked *short* grain rice
		Fresh dried seaweed
Vinegar Sauce:		
½ C.	(120ml.)	Vinegar
1/3 C.	(80ml.)	Honey
1½ tsp.	(7.5ml.)	Salt

1. **Prepare the rice.**
2. **Make the sauce.**
   a. Combine the vinegar, honey and salt in a stainless steel saucepan.
   b. Bring to boil and remove from heat.
3. Combine rice and sauce while both are hot.
4. You may serve these plain or you may add chopped cooked carrots, peas, mushrooms, celery or cucumber.
5. You may also serve them the authentic way by rolling the rice mixture on a sushi mat or waxed paper.
6. Place a sheet of dried seaweed on the mat or waxed paper.
7. Spread the rice on the seaweed to within ½" of the edges.
8. You may roll without filling or add fish, scrambled egg, pickled ginger, or vegetables sliced in thin strips.
9. Hold paper or mat and roll seaweed and rice into a tight roll. Keep as tightly rolled as possible.
10. Cut rolls into 1" thick sections. It helps to dip knife in hot water before each slice.
11. Serve with soy sauce.

TEMPURA

Tempura is a delightful and special dish of Japan that was brought to their culture by the Portuguese. The Japanese adapted and perfected the technique to create a unique dish of their own.

To make it, vegetables are cut imaginatively so that when dipped in the batter and deep fried, each texture and subtle flavor can be appreciated. The secret to successful tempura lies with the batter and the oil. The batter must be fresh, made after the vegetables are cut and the oil heated. Cornstarch or mochi rice flour makes the batter lighter and crisper and more authentic, however, regular flour may be used. The water should be ice-cold for an authentic light batter.

Batter:

1 Tbs.	(15ml.)	Egg
3 Tbs.	(45ml.)	Flour
½ tsp.	(2.5ml.)	Salt
1 Tbs.	(15ml.)	Ice-cold water

Vegetables:

Carrots

Zucchini

Parsley sprigs

Others (Onions, snow peas, broccoli, etc.)

1. Prepare the vegetables in small decorative pieces.
2. Preheat oil to 350°F, 176°C.
3. Prepare batter by:
   a. Beating the egg in a margarine tub.
   b. Adding the flour, salt and ice water. mixing well until smooth. (Do not overstir).
4. Dip vegetables in batter with slotted spoon, then slide them into deep hot oil.
5. Remove from oil when golden brown, drain on paper towels.
6. Serve with soy sauce.

TSUKEMONO (JAPANESE PICKLES)

Japanese pickles are served at nearly every meal, even breakfast. They are beneficial in the aiding of digestion, especially after the eating of fried foods and rice. Many different vegetables are pickled under pressure in a special jar called a tsukemono-ki.

¼ C.	(60ml.)	Salt
½ C.	(120ml.)	Sugar
1 Tbs.	(15ml.)	White vinegar
3 C.	(720ml.)	Boiling water
2 lbs.	(900gms.)	Chinese celery or cabbage

1. Mix the salt, sugar, vinegar and water together, stir until the salt and sugar have dissolved.
2. Cut the cabbage in half through the heart, and then in half again.
3. Soak the cabbage in the solution for one to one and a half days.
4. Remove from the solution, drain and refrigerate.
5. To serve, cut the cabbage into 1" sections. Serve with soy sauce.

THE COOKING OF MEXICO

Mexican cooking today has been influenced by the Aztec, Spanish, and to a lesser extent, French cultures. When the conquistadores came to the Americas, they found foods previously unknown to them: chocolate, vanilla, corn, chilies, tomatoes, avocados, squash, beans, sweet potatoes, pineapple, and papaya. The conquistadores added the oil, wine, spices, rice, wheat, and cattle important to their cuisine and some culinary contributions from Europe, Asia and Arab countries (since Spain was just free from Arab domination). Later, during the reign of Maximilian, French dishes were introduced.

The typical Mexican day begins with desayuno (breakfast), usually a sweet bread with cafe con leche (milk coffee) or chocolate. Then almuerzo, a heartier second breakfast, is eaten about 9:00 a.m. (including fruit or juices, beans, and tortillas). In the city, Almuerzo (lunch) follows at approximately 11:30 a.m. The comida, main meal of the day, takes place anywhere from 2:00 to 5:30 p.m. At night there is the merienda, which is eaten by children at 6:00 to 7:00 p.m. or by adults as late as 9:00 p.m. and is a light meal. Cena is a dinner on a special occasion that is eaten at any time between 8:00 p.m. to midnight. This cena is a meal that closely follows the Spanish eating pattern.

BROWN SUGAR CANDY (DULCE DE PILONCILLO)

Most Mexicans like their candy really sweet. In the market places and in the streets at fiestas, you will see vendors carrying trays high overhead, heaped with thick squares of colored creamy candy.

½ C.	(120ml.)	Brown sugar
2 Tbs.	(30ml.)	Water
¾ tsp.	(3.7ml.)	Vinegar
¾ tsp.	(3.7ml.)	Butter
¼ C.	(60ml.)	Broken pecans or walnuts

1. Mix the brown sugar, water, vinegar and butter in a saucepan.
2. Stir and cook over low heat about fifteen minutes until mixture spins a thread when dropped from a spoon into cold water.
3. Add the nuts.
4. Remove the mixture from the heat and beat until creamy.
5. Drop from a spoon onto waxed paper and allow to cool.

This recipe makes about 5 candies.

BUTTERCAKES (MANTICADOS)

In ancient Mexico, cakes were not prepared because people did not have wheat flour, sugar or butter. A typical dessert was sweet tamales stuffed with fruit. These buttercakes are a sweet enjoyed by Mexican children today.

INGREDIENTS:

2½ Tbs.	(40ml.)	Butter or margarine
2½ Tbs.	(40ml.)	Sugar
1		Egg
1/3 C.	(80ml.)	Flour, sifted
1 tsp.	(5ml.)	Powdered sugar

1. Cream together butter and sugar.
2. Add eggs and beat.
3. Add flour gradually.
4. Beat until smooth.
5. Pour into two dozen muffin tins lined with paper cups.
6. Sprinkle with powdered sugar.
7. Bake at 375°F, 190°C fifteen to twenty minutes.

CHIMICHANGAS (DEEP FRIED FILLED TORTILLAS)

A common variation of the taco or quesadilla is a regional dish from the state of Sonora called Chimichangas.

6		Flour tortillas (7" diameter)
1 C.	(240ml.)	Meat filling (recipe follows)

Filling:

½ lb.	(225gm.)	Lean ground beef
1 Tbs.	(15ml.)	Oil or lard
¼ C.	(60ml.)	Onion, chopped
1 Tbs.	(15ml.)	Red chili sauce

How to mix filling:

1. In frying pan, brown the beef, adding oil or lard if needed.
2. Add onion and cook until soft.
3. Moisten with red chili sauce.
4. Slowly simmer for ten minutes.

How to complete chimichangas:

1. Spoon 3 Tbs. (45ml.) filling down center of tortilla.
2. Roll tortilla around filling and fasten with a toothpick.
3. Fry in 1" of hot oil over medium heat (about 350°F, 176°C) turning until golden.
4. Drain on paper towels.

CHURROS

These fried batter cakes are named after the churro, a Spanish sheep with long, coarse hair. They are sold in market places from small portable cooking stalls called churrerias (churro shops) where they go straight from the fry pan to the customer. In Mexico, the churros have a distinctive flavor because cut-up lime is heated in the cooking oil.

Oil for frying		
One lime or lemon, quartered		
Pinch of salt		
1/3 C.	(80ml.)	Water
1 tsp.	(5ml.)	Sugar
½ C.	(120ml.)	Flour
1 Tbs.	(15ml.)	Egg

1. Preheat oil and lime or lemon pieces to 390°F, 200°C.
2. Combine the water, salt and sugar in a saucepan and heat just to boiling.
3. Add the flour and beat until smooth.
4. Add the egg and beat until mixture is smooth and satiny.
5. Remove lime or lemon pieces from oil.
6. Force the mixture through a pastry tube or large funnel.
7. Fry in long strips until golden.
8. Drain on paper towels.
9. Cut into 3" (7.5 cm.) pieces.
10. Roll in granulated sugar.

 FLAN (MEXICAN CUSTARD)

This dessert of Spanish origin is made in custard cups so that when it is unmolded it is covered with a caramel glaze.

2 Tbs.	(30ml.)	Sugar
1		Egg
3 Tbs.	(45ml.)	Sugar
½ C.	(120ml.)	Milk

1. Heat and stir 2 Tbs. (30ml.) sugar in a saucepan over low heat until it becomes brown and syrupy (caramelized).
2. Pour into a custard cup, covering the bottom and sides.
3. In a bowl beat the egg, 3 Tbs. (45ml.) sugar and the milk. Make sure they are thoroughly mixed.
4. Pour into the baking dish over the caramel.
5. Bake in a 350°F, 176°C oven or electric skillet 35 to 40 minutes.
6. Test by inserting a knife. When the custard is done, the knife comes out clean.
7. Allow the custard to cool.
8. To serve, place a plate over the custard, quickly turn it out upside down on the plate. Custards may be baked in four individual cups.

MEXICAN CHOCOLATE

Chocolate is a historical pre-Columbian drink that in the past was only enjoyed by the king, merchant nobility, and the upper ranks of the priesthood and military. Its name comes from two Nahuatl words, "Xoco", meaning bitter, and "atl", meaning water. It is served in many ways. Sometimes it is sweetened with honey and flavored with vanilla. It is always beaten with a "molinillo" (a small wooden beater that is twirled between the palms).

Mexican children today enjoy "chocolate" and when they use the "molinillo" to mix their chocolate they sometimes sing this song:

Uno — dos — tres cho
Uno — dos — tres co
Uno — dos — tres la
Uno — dos — tres te
Cho —co — la — te
Bate bate
Cho — co — la — te

1 oz.	(30ml.)	Unsweetened chocolate
1 C.	(240ml.)	Cold water
		Honey to taste
		Vanilla to taste

1. Mix the ingredients to taste.
2. Stir with the molinillo (a wire whisk or electric blender may be used.)
3. Sing song while mixing.

55

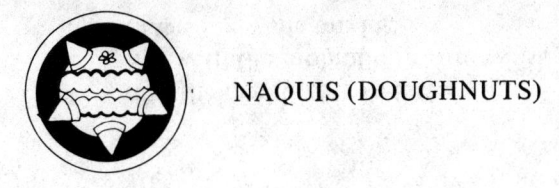

NAQUIS (DOUGHNUTS)

Another kind of deep fried cake similar to churros.

(Note to Mom: please mix together well 1/3 C. (80ml.) buttermilk and one egg.)

½ C.	(120ml.)	Flour, sifted
1/8 tsp.	(.6ml.)	Salt
Small pinch		Baking soda
2 Tbs.	(30ml.)	Sugar
1½ Tbs.	(22.5ml.)	Buttermilk-egg mixture
		Fat for deep frying
		Cinnamon and sugar for coating

1. Mix all the ingredients together to form a soft dough.
2. Add more milk if necessary.
3. Roll and shape into tiny doughnuts, or into cigar shapes.
4. Fry in hot deep fat 350°F, 176°C.
5. Drain on paper towels.

PASTELITOS DE BODA (WEDDING CAKES)

These easy-to-make, delicious cookies are also known as Bride's Cookies or Wedding Cakes.

¼ C.	(60ml.)	Flour, sifted
2 Tbs.	(30ml.)	Butter or margarine
1½ tsp.	(7.5ml.)	Sugar
		A few grains of salt
¼ tsp.	(1.2ml.)	Vanilla
¼ C.	(60ml.)	Finely-ground pecans or walnuts
		Powdered sugar

1. Cream butter and sugar.
2. Add flour, salt, flavoring and nutmeats.
3. Mix well.
4. Form into small balls and place on a lightly greased cookie sheet.
5. Bake in a hot oven 400°F, 204°C for ten minutes or until very lightly browned.
6. Remove from oven and cool slightly, about three minutes.
7. Roll immediately in powdered sugar; repeat when cold.

QUESADILLAS

Quesadillas are another kind of snack. The ingredients and cooking method of quesadillas vary widely depending on the local taste of the region. They get their name from the Spanish word for cheese which is queso. The boiled, white cheese of Oaxaca is the number-one queso of the country; therefore, we recommend Jack cheese for this recipe. Cheddar cheese and corn tortillas are also quite good prepared this way.

1 to 2 Tbs.   (15-30 ml.)

One corn or flour tortilla
Jack cheese (grated) — or any mild, semi-dry white cheese

1. Preheat greased skillet to 375°F, 190°C.
2. Fill tortilla with cheese.
3. Fold over tortilla.
4. Fry quesadilla on both sides until cheese melts.

 **SALTED PEPITAS**

Mexicans enjoy the crunchy nut-like pumpkin seeds, or pepitas. Roasted, they are a good salad garnish or protein-rich snack.

1¼ C.	(300ml.)	Water
2 Tbs.	(30ml.)	Salt
½ lb.	(225gm.)	Untreated hulled pumpkin seeds

1. Boil water and salt for five minutes.
2. Pour water over seeds.
3. Let stand at room temperature overnight.
4. Drain.
5. Place on cookie sheet.
6. Bake at 325°F, 165°C for 40 minutes, stirring occasionally.
7. Cool. Store in an air-tight container.

TACOS

The word "taco" actually means a "snack". In popular usage it has come to mean a particular dish. The word now means a sandwich type of snack with meat filling, garnish and spicy sauce. Sometimes the tortillas are folded in half, often they are rolled all the way around the filling, depending on the region.

One | | | Tortilla
1 Tbs. | (15ml.) | | Precooked, shredded or ground meat (beef, pork, or chicken)

One — Tortilla
1 Tbs. (15ml.) — Precooked, shredded or ground meat (beef, pork, or chicken)
Shredded lettuce
Chopped tomatoes
Grated cheese
Optional: cilantro (Mexican or Chinese parsley)
Salsa (Mexican sauce used in many dishes, sometimes too spicy for children)

1. Preheat oil in fry pan for cooking tortillas.
2. If the child chooses to have tortilla folded in half, have him place tortilla in oil, fry lightly on one side, turn over and fold in half with tongs.
3. Fry both sides of tortilla to desired crispness.
4. Drain on paper towel.
5. Fill with meat and desired condiments.
6. If rolled taco is preferred, have the child place the meat in the tortilla and roll before frying.

 **TORTILLAS**

In Mexico, corn is ground into flour and mixed with water to create a soft flat bread which is eaten plain or may be filled with some other food and rolled and eaten.

Every culture has its own type of bread. Each bread has some common and some different elements depending on the culture and the climate where the group of people live.

| 4 Tbs. | (60ml.) | Masa Harina (corn flour) |
| 3 Tbs. | (45ml.) | Water |

1. Mix the Masa Harina and water. Knead to make dough more pliable.
2. Roll into two balls.
3. Flatten by hand or press on wax paper.
4. Brush skillet with oil and fry briefly on both sides.

THE COOKING OF NATIVE AMERICANS

California's Native Americans cooked and ate what was readily accessible near their home. Their diets included berries, nuts, corn, meat (especially small game), shellfish, locusts, grasshoppers, acorns, and seeds.

On the plains, there were farmers and they used corn as their staple food. In California, they didn't have to farm because all their natural resources were plentiful. Acorns were used in the same manner that the Native Americans of the plains used corn. After they ground the acorns and leached the tannic acid from the meal, they used the acorn to make mush and bread.

The natives of the plains were very innovative farmers and developed many methods used today for fertilizing and crop rotation. We can also thank them for the hybrid corn that we eat today. The early corn was very primitive and through selective planting they developed the corn we enjoy today.

In California, Native Americans cooked in a simplified manner. For example, to boil water they would simply drop red-hot stones into the water. After the water started to boil they would drop in food and more hot rocks.

It is difficult to cook exactly as the Native Americans did because many of their food items are not easily available today and many of them we would not enjoy eating.

 ATOLE

      Seven kinds of oak trees grow wild in the California area. These produce seven distinctly different tastes of acorns with varying degrees of bitterness. To leach out the bitterness (tannic acid) Native Americans would crack the acorns between two rocks and grind the acorns to a powder. They would then pour boiling water through the acorn meal and a fibrous material in order to leach out the tannic acid.

2 Tbs.	(30ml.)	Masa
½ C.	(120ml.)	Water — add a little at a time
1 pinch		Salt

1. Mix the masa, a little warm water and salt.
2. Form a smooth paste and thin with remaining water.
3. Boil 10 minutes over low heat. Stir constantly. Serve.

 BEEF JERKY

Native Americans utilized this slow-drying process to preserve some of their meat. Beef jerky is most easily done as a group activity. Marination and drying are difficult for individual portions.

1½ lbs.	(680gms.)	Flank steak
½ C.	(120ml.)	Soy sauce
1 tsp.	(5ml.)	Liquid smoke (optional)
1 tsp.	(5 ml.)	Seasoned salt
1 C.	(240ml.)	Water
½ tsp.	(2.5ml.)	Garlic salt
½ tsp.	(2.5ml.)	Celery salt
¼ tsp.	(1.2ml.)	Pepper

1. Freeze the flank steak for about one hour. Cut into thin strips.
2. Marinate in sauce overnight. To make sauce, mix the last seven ingredients above.
3. Cover oven rack with foil and make little troughs between rungs for excess juice to drain. Lay strips on rack.
4. Bake at 140°F, 60°C for six to eight hours.
5. To store: do not use airtight container.

CORN

Corn was an important part of the diet for many Native Americans. Originally corn was much smaller and was shaped somewhat like a pine cone. Each of the kernels was completely enclosed in a tough, pointed husk. The Native Americans used ingenuity and selective planting to produce better crops.

Native Americans did not grind their entire corn crop. The ripe ears were eaten as a vegetable, being boiled with the husks on. They also ate the tassels which are rich in protein. Popcorn was also cultivated and it was used both for eating and decoration. Husks were used to make floor mats and woven decorative items.

Only in the New World does the word "corn" refer specifically to maize. Throughout most of the world, corn has been used as a descriptive term to describe the grain common to the area. Columbus and his crew reported to the Santa Maria that the Native Americans had a sort of grain called mahiz. The scientific name for maize is Zea Mays. (Zea is the Greek word for grain; mays is derived from makiy. Makiy is the word for corn in the language of Tainos — an extinct tribe of Native Americans.)

CORNMEAL BREAD

¼ C.	(60ml.)	Cornmeal
1 pinch		Salt
Stir while adding:		
1 Tbs.	(15ml.)	Bacon grease
2 Tbs.	(30ml.)	Boiling water

1. Mix the cornmeal and salt.
2. Stir while adding the grease and boiling water.
3. Use hands to shape dough into small rolls the shape of hot dogs.
4. Wrap rolls in fresh cornhusks. Dampened parchment paper or well-greased wrapping paper may be substituted for cornhusks.
5. Bake at 350°F, 176°C for six minutes.

 CORNMEAL CRISPS

¼ C.	(60ml.)	Cornmeal
2 Tbs.	(30ml.)	Flour
1 pinch		Salt
1 Tbs.	(15ml.)	Melted butter
2 Tbs.	(30ml.)	Milk

1. Sift together the cornmeal, flour and salt.
2. Add the melted butter and milk.
3. Stir. Knead. Divide into 4 balls.
4. Flatten balls and place on ungreased cookie sheet.
5. Bake at 350°F, 176°C for 12-15 minutes. When done, crisps should be lightly browned around edges.

FRUIT LEATHER

Native Americans ground berries on a stone, allowed it to dry, and then removed the dried sheet of sweet-tasting fruit. This substance would not easily spoil; therefore, they could enjoy this delicacy for a longer period of time.

1. Fruit should be at room temperature.
2. Wrap top of cardboard square (approximately 6x6") in plastic wrap.
3. Wash fruit and remove blemishes, skins, and pits. Fruit may be overripe if unspoiled.
4. Puree fruit with sieve or masher. A blender may also be used. Add sweetener, if desired, according to fruit type as listed under "Special Directions for Specific Fruits".
5. Spread puree over plastic wrap, leaving margin at edges.
6. Dry in hot sun until fruit leather feels dry, yet tacky. A thin curtain or screen may be used to keep bugs away. To speed drying, you may cover the leather with more plastic wrap and flip it to dry other side. Another quick way to dry fruit leather is in a closed car sitting in direct sunlight.
7. When dry and tacky roll up in plastic wrap.
8. Store in airtight container.

SPECIAL DIRECTIONS FOR SPECIFIC FRUITS:

Apple: Use early summer apples rather than crisp, hard apples. Add ¼ tsp. cinnamon and ½ C. shredded coconut to 2 C. puree.

Apricots: Do not peel. Add 1 Tbs. honey to each cup puree. Do not chill fruit.

Berry: Wash and hull. Sweeten to taste.

Peach: Peel. Sweetening is optional. Cinnamon may be added.

Pear: Peel. Do not add sweetener.

Plum: Add 1 Tbs. honey to 1 C. puree.

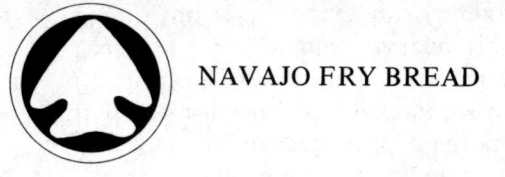 NAVAJO FRY BREAD

This bread was often cooked on a flat black stone, called a soapstone, that can withstand heat and was used much like we use frying pans today.

Sift:

¼ C.	(60ml.)	Flour
1 pinch		Baking powder/salt mix (combined 2:1)

Add:

2 Tbs.	(30ml.)	Lukewarm water

1. Sift the flour, baking powder and salt mixtures.
2. Add the lukewarm water.
3. Combine and knead.
4. Roll out and cut into four 2" squares (about ¼" thick).
5. Brown by turning in hot shortening in electric skillet.
6. Drain on paper towel.
7. Serve hot with jam or honey.

 PEKEE BREAD

The Native Americans of several different groups were known to make a form of Pekee or paper bread. They cooked it on flat stones, which they laid over their fire. For daily eating, the bread was sometimes mixed with ashes and looked grey. On special occasions they would color the bread red by adding small amounts of red dirt. Pekee bread was often rolled to use as an eating utensil to scoop up their stew, similar to the way Mexicans use tortillas.

Mix:

1 Tbs.	(15ml.)	Rye flour
1 Tbs.	(15ml.)	Corn flour
Pinch		4:1 baking powder and salt mixture.

Add:

2 tsp.	(10ml.)	Milk
1 tsp.	(5ml.)	Corn oil

1. Stir well. This should form a thin paste that may be poured onto the griddle.
2. Cook in lightly greased electric skillet 350°F, 176°C, for five to ten minutes.
3. Turn with spatula. Serve with berry jam.

PEMMICAN

Pemmican is a tasty variation on a combination of dried foods.

1 C.	(240ml.)	Ground beef jerky
1 C.	(240ml.)	Beef suet
3 oz.	(50ml.)	Dried raisins or berries
3 oz.	(50ml.)	Dried shelled sunflower seeds

1. Melt suet over low heat.
2. Pour suet over ground jerky and mix with dried fruit and seeds.
3. Cool. Pack in sausage casing or a plastic bag.

TSE ASTE (BREAD COOKED ON A STONE)

This bread was often cooked on a flat black stone called a soapstone that can withstand heat and was used much like we use frying pans today.

3 Tbs.	(45ml.)	Cornmeal
1 pinch		Salt
½ C.	(120ml.)	Boiling water

1. Combine cornmeal and salt.
2. Add the boiling water.
3. Grease soapstone griddle or electric skillet at 350°F, 176°C with small piece of mutton tallow or bacon fat.
4. Preheat griddle until a drop of water sizzles when placed upon it.
5. Stir batter frequently. Measure by tablespoons onto griddle.
6. Cook until bread is crisp and loosened at the edges.
7. Turn with spatula to crisp other side.

THE COOKING OF WESTERN AFRICA

Just as foods vary from region to region in the United States, they also vary in Africa. Foods depend largely upon the climate and what foods are available in that region. Peanuts and peanut butter are major foods throughout much of Africa. There are 49 countries in Africa and many cultures have influenced African cooking.

The African mother cooks for her entire family including friends and in-laws. According to African custom, one must invite all visitors to join in a meal. Frequently, the African meal is served to as many as twenty persons.

In our research we came across this African proverb, "Come into my home. Sit at my table; then you will know me."

72

 **AKARA (BLACK-EYED PEA FRITTERS)**

In Africa these fritters are often passed with a tomato-base hot sauce.

½ lb. or 1¼ C.	(300ml.)	Dried black-eyed peas
¼ C.	(60ml.)	Chopped onion
1 Tbs.	(15ml.)	Ginger root, scraped
½ to 3/4 C.	(120-180ml.)	Water (½ C. then more by Tbs.)
¼ tsp.	(1.2ml.)	Red pepper
1 tsp.	(5ml.)	Salt
		Vegetable oil for frying

1. Soak the peas in hot water.
2. Loosen and remove the skins with your hands.
3. Drain and repeat.
4. In a blender, combine the remaining ingredients and the cleaned peas and blend for 30 seconds at high speed.
5. Transfer the puree to a bowl and beat three to four minutes until light and fluffy.
6. Take a small handful of the mixture and make fritter to be fried.
7. Deep fat fry in vegetable oil at 375°F, 190°C for five minutes or until golden brown.

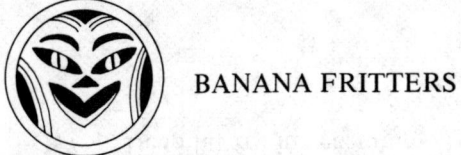

BANANA FRITTERS

Another recipe that can be compared to potato pancakes, Japanese egg rolls, or any fritter.

½ C.	(120ml.)	All-purpose flour
2 Tbs.	(30ml.)	Sugar
1		Egg
1/3 C.	(80ml.)	Milk
One half		Very ripe banana, peeled and mashed

1. Combine flour and sugar.
2. Add egg and milk.
3. Add the peeled and mashed bananas.
4. Form the fritters.
5. Deep fat fry at 375°F, 190°C for three minutes to a rich golden brown.
6. Drain on paper towel.
7. Sprinkle with confectioners sugar.

CASSAVA CHIPS

These chips are much like Greek drachma fried potatoes or potato chips.

One large cassava or yam		
1 C.	(240ml.)	Oil

1. Peel the cassava.
2. Cut paper-thin slices of the cassava with a potato peeler.
3. Fry in deep fat until golden brown.
4. Drain on paper towel and sprinkle with salt. 74

FRIED PLANTAIN (BANANA FINGERS)

Cooks on the Ivory Coast use the plentiful plantain in their everyday cooking. There are many ways to use the plantain. It can be prepared as an accompaniment to meat or fish or as a dessert.

Two plantains or four bananas
Lemon juice
Peanut oil (about 1/3 C., 80ml.)
Crushed corn flakes or bread crumbs
Pepper or powdered sugar

1. Cut bananas into quarters lengthwise and then into halves crosswise.
2. Cover with lemon juice for ten minutes.
3. Roll in the crumbs.
4. Fry quickly in ½ inch of peanut oil until crispy brown.
5. Sprinkle with pepper or powdered sugar.

FUFU (CASSAVA BALLS)

The cassava is the staple food of many western African countries. It is prepared in a variety of ways. One possibility is the following.

1		Large cassava or yam
1		Egg
5 Tbs.	(75ml.)	Evaporated milk
1		Onion, grated
Pinch		Garlic salt
3 Tbs.	(45ml.)	Butter or margarine

1. Peel and cut the cassava or yam into small pieces.
2. Boil pieces until tender in ½ C. (120ml.) water approximately twenty minutes.
3. Drain off the water and mash until smooth.
4. Add the egg, milk, onion and garlic salt.
5. Beat and roll into 2" balls. If the mixture is too wet add a little flour.
6. Fry in butter until brown.

GHANA CAKES

In Ghana, these delicious cakes are served at receptions and parties. Another name for them is twisted cakes. They are really more like doughnuts than like cakes.

(Ask your mom to beat well 1 egg and 1 C. (240 ml.) milk together for the egg-milk mixture below.)

1 Tbs.	(15ml.)	Shortening
2 Tbs.	(30ml.)	Sugar
¼ C.	(60ml.)	Flour
2 tsp.	(10ml.)	Milk and egg mixture
		Fat for deep frying

1. Cream together the shortening and the sugar.
2. Add the flour and mix well.
3. Add the 2 tsp. (10ml.) milk and egg mixture and mix well.
4. Form the dough into approximately ten balls.
5. Fry in deep fat until golden brown.
6. Drain on paper towels.

GROUNDNUT SOUP (GHANA PEANUT SOUP)

Ghana is an exporter of peanuts and also uses them frequently in their cooking. A typical example of their use of peanuts is groundnut soup.

1		Chicken, cut up
1		Onion, chopped
1 can	(480ml.)	Tomatoes
1 C.	(240ml.)	Peanut butter
		Water
		Ground red pepper to taste, if desired

1. Brown the chicken and onions in a large saucepan until golden.
2. Add just enough cold water to cover the chicken and add tomatoes and salt to taste.
3. Bring to boil, lower heat and simmer for fifteen minutes.
4. Mix the peanut butter into a smooth cream with some of the hot stock.
5. Pour this creamed paste into the saucepan.
6. Cook slowly until the oil rises to the top of the soup.
   This recipe serves six.

LIBERIAN RICE BREAD

Liberia was founded in 1821 for the resettling of freed Black people. Since then they have cultivated their own rice, sugar cane, and cassava. Rice is their staple food and is eaten at least twice a day.

2 C.	(480ml.)	Cream of rice
3 Tbs.	(45ml.)	Sugar
4 tsp.	(20ml.)	Baking powder
½ tsp.	(2.5ml.)	Salt
One and one half		Mashed plantains or bananas
2		Eggs
1½ C.	(360ml.)	Milk
1 C.	(240ml.)	Oil

1. Grease a 8x12" pan.
2. Preheat oven to 375°F, 190°C.
3. Mix dry ingredients.
4. Gradually add bananas, eggs and milk.
5. Add oil and blend thoroughly.
6. Pour into the well-greased pan.
7. Bake at 375°F, 190°C for 45 minutes.

INDEX